To

_____

From

_____

Text by Sophie Piper
Illustrations copyright © 2007 Angelo Ruta
This edition copyright © 2013 Lion Hudson

The right of Angelo Ruta to be identified as
the illustrator of this work has been asserted
by him in accordance with the Copyright,
Designs and Patents Act 1988.

Published by Lion Children's Books
an imprint of
Lion Hudson plc
Wilkinson House, Jordan Hill Road,
Oxford OX2 8DR, England
www.lionhudson.com/lionchildrens

ISBN 978 0 7459 6367 9

First edition 2013

Acknowledgments

Bible extracts are taken or adapted from
the Good News Bible published by the Bible
Societies and HarperCollins Publishers,
© American Bible Society 1994, used with
permission.

The Lord's Prayer (on page 31) as it
appears in *Common Worship: Services and
Prayers for the Church of England* (Church
House Publishing, 2000) is copyright ©
The English Language Liturgical
Consultation and is reproduced by
permission of the publisher.

A catalogue record for this book is available
from the British Library

Printed and bound in China,
November 2012, LH17

The Life of
Jesus

Retold by Sophie Piper ✤ *Illustrated by Angelo Ruta*

LION
CHILDREN'S

Contents

Introduction

Jesus lived some 2,000 years ago, at the time of the Roman empire. He was born and raised in an ordinary working family in the region of Galilee. He became a preacher and was, for a short time, hugely popular with the crowds. However, the religious authorities of his people, the Jews, disapproved of his teaching. They plotted to have him put to death, and their scheming led to him being crucified on the orders of the Roman governor, Pontius Pilate.

That might have been the end, and Jesus' life would have faded into obscurity. Yet something gave his followers the courage to keep his message alive.

Three days after he was laid in a tomb, they claimed they had seen him alive. This resurrection confirmed what they already believed: that Jesus was God's Son, born on earth to restore the friendship between God and people. Those who believed in him would be allowed into the presence of the one who is holy and perfect, forgiven of all their flaws and failings.

They believed he was the king promised by the prophets of ancient times: the Hebrew word for this king was messiah; the Greek word was Christ. Soon, those who believed that Jesus was the Christ became known as Christians.

It was those followers who had known Jesus who first spread the message. As the number of believers grew, they wanted to know more about Jesus' life. Of the accounts that were written, four have been included in the Bible: the Gospels of Matthew, Mark, Luke, and John.

It is from them that Christians today know about the life of Jesus: the life that has inspired the Christian faith.

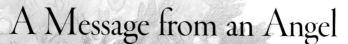

A Message from an Angel

Luke 1:26-56

LONG AGO, IN
the time of the
Roman empire,
lived a young
woman named
Mary. Her home
was Nazareth: a town
nestled among the fields
and hills of Galilee. There she had
grown up and there she was expecting
to stay when she married Joseph — as
soon she would.

One day, the angel Gabriel came to
Mary with a message from God.

"Greetings from heaven," said the
angel. "God has chosen you to be the
mother of a child — God's own Son,

Jesus. He will be a king, bringing God's blessing to the world."

Mary gasped. "That can't be!" she exclaimed. "I'm not yet married."

"God can do anything," replied the angel. "Think about your cousin Elizabeth. No one thought she would ever have a baby, but she's now six months pregnant."

"That's true," said Mary thoughtfully. "And I have always tried to obey God in everything. So yes!"

Even as Mary looked up with a smile, the angel vanished. What was Mary to do now?

"I'll go and visit Elizabeth," she said to herself. "Surely she will understand."

When Mary arrived, Elizabeth rushed to hug her. "I felt the baby inside me jump for joy when I heard your voice," she said.

Mary told her cousin her astonishing news, and as she did so happiness bubbled out of her.

"God is wonderful and amazing and holy and kind. Thank you, God, for choosing me to do your will. Thank you, God, for keeping your promise to bless the world."

The Birth of Jesus

Luke 1:46-56 and 2:1-7

THE MORE MARY pondered what the angel had said, the more astonished she grew.

"Our holy writings tell of God's promise to our people – to bless the poor, to humble the wealthy, to set our people free.

"And all this could come true through my son!"

Perhaps it could: but for now the people were not free. A reminder that they were ruled by the Romans came in an announcement from the emperor Augustus himself.

"Everyone must go to their home town. There they are to register as taxpayers."

Mary looked anxious as Joseph explained exactly what that meant.

"My family can trace its roots back to King David of long ago. My home town is Bethlehem.

"I know it's not a good time to make a long journey, what with the baby due. But we have little choice."

It took several days for Mary and Joseph to journey from Nazareth to Bethlehem. They arrived to find the town crowded. The only room they could find was one they had to share with the animals.

There, where the oxen lowed and the donkey stamped and shuffled, Mary's baby, Jesus, was born. She wrapped him in swaddling clothes and laid him in the manger.

13

Shepherds and Angels

Luke 2:8-20

OUT ON THE hills near Bethlehem, some shepherds huddled together. The night was cold. From the fold, one of the lambs bleated, its treble voice answered by a low, maternal baa.

The men were grumbling idly. "Taxes going up soon, I hear," said one.

"Just to keep a foreign emperor in luxury," added a second.

"What we need is real change," added a third, and the others nodded.

As they sat, a sudden blaze of light scattered the darkness. From its centre, a voice called out.

"I bring good news!" cried the angel. "Tonight, in Bethlehem's royal city, a new king has been born. Go and find him: God's promised king, wrapped in swaddling clothes and lying in a manger."

Then the sky was filled with angels singing:

"Glory to God in heaven!
On earth, peace."

For a golden moment, it seemed that heaven and earth were one.
Then the angels vanished.

The shepherds looked at each other in amazement. "Let's go and
see!" they agreed.

In a humble room where a lamp shone from an open window,
they found Mary and Joseph. In the manger was the newborn child,
just as the angel had said.

"We saw angels," they explained. And as they told of all they
had seen and heard, Mary smiled. Surely God's promises were all
coming true.

The Wise Men and the Star

Matthew 2:1-15

THE MEN GAZED in awe at the night-time sky.

"A new star," they agreed, "and a sign that a new king has been born to the Jewish nation. We must go and worship him."

So saying, the wise men set out to travel the long miles to Jerusalem. Their joy at arriving soon turned to dismay. No one had heard of a newborn king. The men were wondering what to do next when a summons arrived. They had to go to the palace and explain themselves to King Herod.

"As you know," Herod told them, and his tone held a hint of threat, "I rule the Jews on behalf of Rome.

"But the Scriptures speak of a messiah who is to come – a king sent by God.

"Now, I have useful information: you need to search for him in Bethlehem. When you find him, report back to me."

The men set out on the Bethlehem road. To their delight, the star they had seen in the east shone on their path. It led them to Jesus.

They presented him with their tribute gifts: gold, frankincense, and myrrh.

The men did not return to Herod. In a dream, an angel warned them that he meant to harm the child.

An angel also spoke to Joseph. "Hurry," said the angel. "Take your family to Egypt. God has chosen you to keep them safe, and it will be some time before you can return home."

The Boy Jesus

Luke 2:41-51

FOR AS LONG as Jesus could really remember, he had lived in
Nazareth. Every year he had waved goodbye as his parents set off
for the Passover festival in Jerusalem. How he longed to join the
group of pilgrims!

At last he was twelve — and allowed to go. Jesus knew all the
Passover stories: how God had rescued the people from slavery and
led them to the land they now called home; how God had made an
agreement with the people, a covenant always to be their God if
they would obey God's laws.

He loved talking about it all.

Then it was time to return
home. At the end of the first
day's journey, Mary began to
look for Jesus among her relatives
and friends.

Jesus wasn't there.

Fearful and anxious, Jesus' parents
hurried back to Jerusalem and began
three days of frantic searching.

Then they found him: Jesus was in
the Temple, talking earnestly with
the wisest rabbis, the teachers who
helped explain the meaning of the
Scriptures.

"Why did you do this?" Mary demanded. "We've been so worried about you!"

"Didn't you know I would be here?" replied Jesus. "This is my Father's house."

Then, without protest, he went back to Nazareth with them, a good and obedient son.

Jesus is Baptized

Mark 1:1-13

DOWN BY THE River Jordan, a crowd of people had gathered.

"That's John preaching," whispered a new arrival to her friend. "Doesn't he look like a prophet of old in that rough old cloak!"

"Well, his father, Zechariah, was a priest," commented her companion. "I wonder what his mother, Elizabeth, makes of it."

"Listen: he's telling people to turn away from all their sinful, wicked ways and be baptized. Lots of people are lining up, aren't they?"

Then John's words rang out more clearly. "I baptize with water as a sign of your new beginning. There is one coming – greater than I am – who will baptize you with God's Holy Spirit."

Not long after, Jesus came and asked to be baptized. As John lifted him out of the water, God's Spirit settled on him in the form of a dove. A voice spoke from heaven:

"You are my Son; I am pleased with you."

For forty days, Jesus went deeper into the desert, thinking of all that lay ahead. "Give up," whispered the forces of evil; but Jesus knew what God had chosen him to do, and angels came to give him strength.

The Work Begins

Luke 4:14-37

FROM THE TIME he was a boy, Jesus had gone to the synagogue in Nazareth every sabbath.

Now he was a man, he would take his turn to read from the Scriptures. On one particular sabbath, he was handed a passage from the book of the prophet Isaiah.

"The Spirit of the Lord is upon me," Jesus read, "because he has chosen me to bring good news to the poor... to announce that the time has come when the Lord will save his people."

He handed back the scroll and sat down.

"Those words have come true today," he said.

The people of Nazareth were furious. "The son of Joseph said what? Does he claim to be a prophet? It's outrageous!"

Jesus fled Nazareth and went to Capernaum on the shores of Lake Galilee. The people there were impressed with the young preacher and willingly invited him to speak.

One day, a man who was known for his odd behaviour came to the synagogue. Suddenly he screamed at Jesus: "I know who you are – you are God's holy messenger, and you have come to destroy us."

"Quiet," said Jesus firmly. His words were not to the man – rather to the power that drove him out of his mind.

The man fell to the ground... and then stood up, healed of his affliction.

At Simon's Home

Luke 4:38-40

SIMON THE FISHERMAN was already becoming a good friend of Jesus.

"Could you come over to my house?" he asked, when the synagogue meeting was over. "My mother-in-law has a really bad fever. I was wondering if you could help."

Jesus went to where the elderly woman lay half asleep in her bed.

"Leave her alone," he said to the fever.

The woman sat up at once. "Oh!" she exclaimed. "A guest in the house. How wonderful. Now you young men sit down and I'll get everything ready."

By sunset, news of how Jesus had made her well had spread. From all over Capernaum people came, bringing with them those in need of healing. Jesus healed them all.

Jesus and the Fishermen

Luke 5: 1-11

ONE DAY, JESUS began preaching down by the shore of Lake Galilee. A huge crowd gathered, eager to hear his every word.

Jesus turned to where some young fishermen were sitting by their boats washing out their nets.

"Simon," he called to his friend. "Can I sit in your boat, and you push just a little way out on the water?"

Simon agreed, and Jesus continued preaching. When he had finished, he called to Simon again.

"Push the boat into deeper water now so you can catch some fish."

"It's not worth the bother," replied Simon. "We fished all night and caught nothing."

"Try it and see," said Jesus.

Simon shrugged and did as Jesus asked. To his astonishment, the nets filled with fish.

"Over here," he called to the others. "I need help."

Simon and his friends James and John needed all their strength to bring the catch to shore. Simon fell to his knees. "Jesus," he said, "you go your way; I'm not good enough to be part of it."

"Don't be afraid," said Jesus. "I've watched how skilfully you bring fish to shore. From now on, I want you all to join me in bringing people into God's kingdom."

The men left their nets and went with Jesus. They were his first disciples.

Preaching on the Hillside

Matthew 5, 6

JESUS LOOKED AT the huge crowds that had gathered to listen to him. He walked up to the top of the hill. From there he began to preach.

"My message," he said, "is for all of you who long to live as friends of God and know you have fallen short. God will bless you. God will welcome you into the kingdom of heaven.

"Up until now, you have had the Law God gave our people long ago to guide you. I haven't come to challenge the Law, but to enable you to obey it fully.

"You have heard it said you should love your friends and hate your enemies. Now I am telling you to love

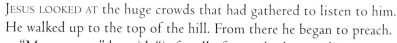

your enemies and pray for those who are unkind to you. Remember that God lets the sun shine and the rain fall on bad people and good people alike. You too must be generous and good to everyone.

"Don't spend your life worrying about possessions and how to get rich. Just look at how God provides food for the wild birds! Admire the beauty of the petals in which God clothes the flowers.

"Make it your aim to live good and holy lives – as friends of God; you can be quite sure that God will take care of everything else."

How to Pray

Matthew 6:5-15

JESUS LOOKED AT the crowds on the hillside. There were all kinds of people there – beggars dressed in rags, well-to-do rabbis, old people who had struggled to walk so far, and children larking around. Jesus knew his message was for all of them.

"God wants all of you to lead good and holy lives," he said. "But it's never right to show off about how good you are so you get lots of thanks and praise. If you do a good deed, do it secretly.

"I'm sure you've noticed the kind of people who say their prayers on street corners – arms uplifted, eyes closed as if thinking of nothing but God. They just want other people to notice and admire. When you pray, go into your room, close the door, and pray to your Father in heaven.

"You don't need lots of clever words. Here is the one prayer you need to know:

"Our Father in heaven,
hallowed be your name,
your kingdom come,
your will be done
on earth as in heaven.
Give us today our daily bread.
Forgive us our sins
as we forgive those who sin against us.
Lead us not into temptation
but deliver us from evil."

"Forgive all those who have wronged you, and then you can be
sure that God in heaven will forgive all the wrong you have done."

The Two House Builders

Matthew 7:11-12, 24-27

"YOU CAN BE sure of this," said Jesus to his listeners. "God is longing to bless you with good things.

"All you need to do to live in obedience to God is to do for others what you would want them to do for you.

"Anyone who follows this teaching is like the wise man: when he decides to build himself a house, he chooses a safe place high on a rock. When the rain comes pouring down, when the river floods and the wind blows a gale, his house is completely safe.

"If you don't pay attention to my teaching, then you are like the foolish man who chooses a plot on the sandy soil beside the river.

"When the rain comes pouring down, when the river floods and the wind blows a gale, the foolish man's house is swept away.

"There is nothing left: nothing."

Water into Wine

John 2:1-11

FOR THIS PARTICULAR wedding, the little town of Cana had become one huge party. The families of the bride and groom had invited everyone they could think of. Jesus was there with his disciples from Capernaum. Jesus' mother Mary had come over from Nazareth. People were eating and drinking, laughing and singing, and those dancing wound their way through the crowd with much stamping and clapping.

In the midst of all this merriment, Mary hurried over to Jesus.

"Dreadful news," she whispered. "They've just run out of wine. The families will be so embarrassed. Please help."

"Only I can decide when to act," replied Jesus. "This isn't my time."

Mary shrugged and hurried over to the servants. "Do whatever my son says," she whispered.

Jesus wandered over. He looked at the huge jars normally used for washing. They were kept very clean. Then he spoke to the servants.

"Can you fill these up with water, please?" he said.

They did so at once, rushing to add one pitcherful after another.

"Now ladle some into a goblet and take it to the master of ceremonies," said Jesus.

The servants did so at once.

The master of ceremonies sniffed at the goblet. He swirled the liquid around. He took a sip.

"Mmm," he said. Then he called to the bridegroom. "I thought we'd be on to the cheap wine by now, but this is the very best."

Nicodemus Asks a Question

John 3:1-21

NICODEMUS WAS PUZZLED. He had spent years studying the Scriptures. His wisdom had won him the respect of many people and he was well regarded among the Pharisees – all of them, like him, devout and sincere men.

But now his confidence in his learning had been shaken.

Nicodemus had heard Jesus preaching. People had told him about Jesus' miracles of healing. He wanted to question Jesus more closely. The other Pharisees might not think well of that… so here he was, in the dark of night, asking to speak to the young preacher privately.

"Your miracles are a clear sign that you are sent by God," began Nicodemus.

Jesus spoke quietly: "No one can see the kingdom of God unless they are born again," he said.

"That's an odd thing to say," said Nicodemus. "No one can be born again. What people did as a baby can't be undone – let alone a lifetime."

"They must be born of God's Holy Spirit," said Jesus. "The Spirit changes people – as mysteriously and as powerfully as the wind changes everything it touches.

"Can you, with all your learning, understand this? God has sent his Son to bring eternal life to those who believe in him. Those who long to live as friends of God will recognize that the Son is the light, showing them the right way to go."

The Hole in the Roof

Mark 2:1-12

"GENTLY," CALLED THE man to his four friends. "Put me down, but gently this time."

The four who had been carrying the man on his sleeping mat sighed.

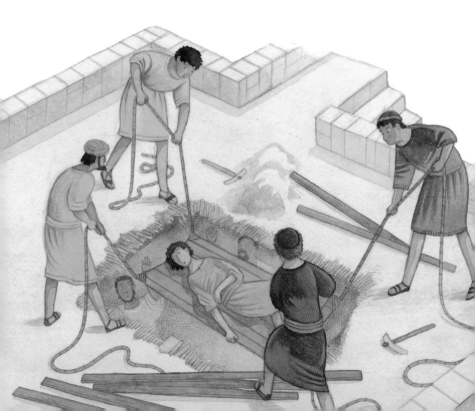

"Apparently Jesus is inside that house there," said one. "It's going to be hard shoving our way through to him."

"Let's think about this differently," said another. "See the stairs to the roof — crumbling at the edges. If the roof is in the same state, it's already in need of repair. Let's make a bit of a trapdoor in it."

Chuckling, the men carried the friend who could not walk right up onto the flat roof. They scrabbled at the plaster. They hacked away until there was a hole. In spite of noisy complaints from the room below, they were soon able to let their friend down on ropes: right to where Jesus was.

Jesus looked up at the men. He saw their faces, full of hope.

He looked at the man on his mat. "Your sins are forgiven," he said.

At once the room filled with whispering. The rabbis were objecting to the words. "Only God can forgive sins," they hissed. "How dare Jesus say that?"

"Which is easier to say," asked Jesus, "'Your sins are forgiven' or 'Get up and walk'? Well, I'll prove to you that I have the authority to forgive sins."

He smiled at the man. "Get up," he said. "Take the mat and go home."

To everyone's amazement, the man who had been carried to Jesus stood up, nodded shyly, and hurried away.

The Sower and the Seed

Luke 8:4-15

FROM ALL THE towns and villages of Galilee, people were gathering to see Jesus. Some sought wisdom; others, an entertaining day out. Some needed a miracle; others doubted that Jesus had any authority from God. Jesus told this parable:

"There was once a man who went out to sow his field. He walked up and down the ploughed earth scattering the seed in great handfuls.

"Some of it fell on the trodden path. Birds swooped down to eat it.

"Some fell on rocky ground. It sprouted well enough, but the young roots had no depth of soil, and the plants soon wilted in the sun.

"Some seed fell among thorn bushes. The seedlings struggled towards the light, but the stronger plants choked them, so they remained yellow and weak.

"Some seed fell on good soil. The plants grew strongly, watered by the rain and ripened by the sun. At harvest time, each produced a full ear of grain – some as many as a hundred new seeds each."

Jesus looked at the crowd: "Are you listening?" he asked. "Do you have ears to hear what I am saying?"

At the end of the day, Jesus' disciples gathered closer. "What did that story mean?" they wanted to know.

Jesus smiled. "The seed in the story is the word of God. Some people are like the seed that lands on the path: they hear the word, but it is snatched away almost at once.

"Others are like the seed that falls on rocky ground: they welcome the message and start to live their lives by it; all too soon they find the going tough, and they give up.

"Others are like the seed that tumbles among thorn bushes. They recognize the value of God's word, but it comes to nothing. Their lives are crowded with all kinds of everyday worries.

"Others are like the seed that settles on the rich and fertile soil. They take God's message deep into their hearts and minds, and it grows within them. As a result, they produce a harvest of good deeds."

Parables of the Kingdom

Matthew 13:31-32, 34-35, 44-46

JESUS OFTEN SPOKE of something he called the kingdom of heaven – God's own kingdom. But what did it mean?

"The kingdom of heaven is like this," Jesus told them. "A man takes a tiny mustard seed and sows it in his field. The seed is just a speck, but it grows into a huge plant. It becomes a tree, and all the birds come and make their nests in it.

"Or you can think of the kingdom of heaven like this. A man is digging in a field when his spade strikes something hidden in the soil. He digs down to uncover it and finds priceless treasure. He is thrilled at the find... but how can he make it his? He hurries off home and sells all he has so that he can buy the field.

"Maybe this story will help you understand. A merchant travels the world looking for fine pearls. He knows real quality when he sees it, and he has a fine collection. Then one day, he is offered the most exquisite pearl he has ever seen: that rarest of finds – perfection itself. He knows exactly what he must do. He goes and sells all his other treasures so that he can have that priceless pearl."

A Storm on the Lake

Mark 4:35-41

THE SUN WAS setting on yet another long day of preaching. Jesus was weary.

"It's time to move on," he said. "Let's all climb aboard the boat and sail across to the other side of Lake Galilee."

The sturdy wooden craft with its square-rigged sail made good progress across the lapping waters, driven on by a steady breeze. Jesus found something to use as a pillow and settled down to sleep in the back of the boat.

Suddenly the boat surged forward. The fishermen glanced at one another. "Here comes one of those evil storms," they said.

In no time, a gusty wind had whipped up the waves. The boat began to pitch and toss, and spray crashed over the sides, as cold and sharp as ice.

"Wake up, Jesus!" they cried.

"We're going to drown if we don't all pull together."

"Do something to help, man!"

Jesus shook himself awake. Steadying himself on the side, he stood up.

"Can you hear me, wind?" he cried. In a whisper he added: "Then hush."

The wind dropped. "And you waves," said Jesus, "lie down; be still."

At once everything was calm.

"What made you so afraid?" Jesus asked his friends. "Have you no faith?"

As he lay down and closed his eyes, the disciples glanced fearfully at one another. "Who is he," they asked, "that even the wind and waves obey him?"

Jairus' Daughter

Mark 5:21-43

DOWN BY THE lakeside, a great crowd had gathered. Their eyes were fixed on a little fishing boat coming steadily to shore.

"Is that Jesus by the mast? No, that's his friend, isn't it? Simon, the one he calls Peter."

"Either Peter or his brother Andrew. And the disciples James and John were fishermen too, weren't they? I don't know if the other disciples can sail a boat."

"We'll soon find out – oh, they're going to land over *there*. Quick, hurry."

Everyone in the crowd was eager to see Jesus, but no one was more desperate than Jairus. As an official at the local synagogue, he normally got some respect from the townsfolk, but today they were all too keen to be at the front of the throng to care.

"Please," said Jairus, "please let me through. My daughter – her illness – no, she isn't better, she's worse. Excuse me, I must get to Jesus."

Jairus paid no attention to the elbowing or the angry looks he got. He pushed his way to the front and fell on his knees. "Rabbi, I need your help. My daughter is dying. Please come and heal her. There's no time to lose."

"Of course I'll come," replied Jesus. "Lead on."

The crowds continued to jostle and it was hard for anyone to move. Jairus was almost weeping with frustration.

And then Jesus stopped. "Who touched me?" he asked.

"What kind of question is that?" laughed Peter, using his considerable strength to prevent more of a crush. "Just about everybody is trying to grab you."

"Someone touched my cloak," he said. "I felt someone trying to reach out for healing."

Jesus would not go on until someone answered. At last a woman came closer and fell at his feet. "It was me," she said. "I've been unwell for years. I've spent all my money on doctors but they've brought no cure."

"Thank you for your faith," said Jesus. "It has made you well."

Even as Jesus was speaking, a messenger came from Jairus' house.

"You don't need to bring the rabbi home now," he said. "I'm afraid… it's too late. She passed away peacefully."

Jairus simply broke down.

"Don't worry," said Jesus. "Have faith."

He beckoned for three disciples to come with him and hurried up the street with Jairus.

From some distance away they heard the sound of wailing. The mourners had already arrived to lament the death in the traditional fashion.

"There's no need for all that," Jesus told them. "The poor girl is only sleeping."

"How dare you say that!" jeered one of the mourners. "You've never laid out a body, have you?"

"Let's go to the room," said Jesus. Jairus and his wife led the way, and Jesus' three disciples followed.

Jesus went to the girl's bedside. "Little girl," he said. "Time to get up."

The girl pulled the sheet away from her face. "Oh," she said. "Was I asleep long? I feel quite hungry."

She was completely well.

The Bread of Life

John 6:1-14, 25-35

JESUS AND HIS disciples were dedicated to spreading the news about God's kingdom. Even so, they needed a rest sometimes, and one day they sailed to a quiet bay of Lake Galilee.

Somehow the crowds worked out where Jesus must be heading. They came hurrying along the shore to find him.

"We shall have to welcome them," said Jesus. "Philip, do you know where we can get food for them?"

Philip shook his head. What was Jesus thinking? There were thousands of people! What would it cost to feed them all?

Then Peter's brother Andrew came along. "There's a young lad who has five loaves and two fish," he said. "He's happy to share… though it's hardly enough."

"Get the people to sit down," said Jesus.

When everyone was settled on the grass, Jesus took the loaves and fishes and said a prayer of thanks. "Now share it out," he told his disciples.

Somehow there was enough food for everyone.

When the meal was over, the disciples gathered up twelve baskets of leftovers. Jesus himself was not to be seen.

The crowd was puzzled about where he might be. It was not until the next day that they found him, back on the other side of the lake.

"I know why you're looking for me," said Jesus. "But you are making a mistake. You want a king. You want miracles. What you should be looking for is the food that will satisfy your soul and spirit."

"What on earth do you mean?" they laughed. "Bread of heaven!"

"I am the bread of life," replied Jesus. "Those who believe in me will never go hungry."

Who is Jesus?

Matthew 16:1-4, 13-18

THE RELIGIOUS LEADERS were worried. Was Jesus really a man of whom God approved? Or was he a fraud, playing fast and loose with their people's most sacred beliefs?

They decided to put Jesus to the test, so they went and asked him to perform a miracle for them. Jesus shook his head.

"You know what they say – 'Red sky at night, shepherd's delight, red sky in the morning, shepherd's warning.'

"You trust weather lore and yet you refuse to see the signs of what is happening in our time. You'll have no proof miracle from me."

Then again, were his own disciples understanding the signs? He took them away from Galilee, to Caesarea Philippi. "Tell me," he said. "Who do people say that I am?"

"Some think you're John the Baptist, back from the dead after his unjust execution."

"Others say you're one of the prophets from the Scriptures. Elijah, even."

"And who do you say that I am?" asked Jesus.

Peter answered at once: "You are the messiah, the Son of the Living God."

Jesus smiled. "An answer inspired by God," he said. "Peter, you are the rock on which I will build my church."

Then a shadow passed over his face. "There are going to be hard times ahead, though," he warned. "You need to be ready to face them."

The Light on the Mountain

Matthew 17:1-19

PETER PAUSED A moment to catch his breath. Jesus was clearly taking them right to the top of the mountain. He glanced behind. James and John had nearly caught up.

"I wonder why he chose us three to come here?" he thought briefly.

He plodded on, his eyes on the rough track. James and John came alongside. "Nearly at the top," they agreed.

As the ground levelled off, they looked up – and gasped. The summit was caught in a shimmering light. Jesus' face shone like gold, and his clothes glowed a pure, bright white. There were two other figures there, and the three were talking together.

"It looks like Moses!" said Peter.

"And Elijah," added John.

"The great prophets of old," agreed James.

Peter rushed forward. "Let's make this a special place," he said. "I could easily put up a shelter for each of you, and then the holiness of this moment will last."

Even as he spoke, a shining cloud enveloped the scene. A voice spoke.

"This is my own dear Son. Listen to him!"

Terrified, the three disciples threw themselves to the ground. When they dared look up, they found themselves alone with Jesus on an open mountaintop.

"Come on," he said. "Don't be afraid."

As the four came down the mountain, Jesus spoke solemnly.

"You are not to say anything about what you saw today," he said. "Not until the Son of Man has been raised from the dead."

Forgiving and Not Forgiving

Matthew 18:21-35

PETER HAD OFTEN heard Jesus talk about the need to forgive others. Now he had an important question.

"If someone keeps on doing wrong, how many times should I forgive? Seven?"

Jesus shook his head. "Seventy times seven," he replied. "The kingdom of heaven is like this:

"There was once a king who decided to check on how much each of his servants owed him. Among the first to be brought before him was a man who owed a fortune.

"'I want that paid back at once!' said the king.

"The man pleaded. 'I just don't have the money.'

"'Then you'll pay for it a different way,' said the king. He turned to a guard. 'Seize his family,' he said. 'He and they can be sold as slaves.'

"'No!' the servant cried. 'Please, don't do that. Wait a while. I'll get the money together.'

"The king felt sorry for the man, and agreed.

"The servant went out. He saw another of the palace staff and remembered he wasn't the only man in debt. He grabbed the hapless servant by the throat. 'That money you owe me,' he snarled. 'I want it now!'

"'I will pay,' said the man, 'truly I will. Just give me the time to get the money together.'

"'I've waited long enough!' said the first servant. He ordered the man to be thrown into jail.

"The other servants soon made sure the king heard of the injustice.

"'You worthless wretch!' he told his servant. 'You should have been as forgiving to others as I was to you.

"'Throw him in jail,' he said to the guard.

"And that," Jesus told Peter, "is how God will treat those who do not forgive."

The Good Samaritan

Luke 10:25-37

THE RABBI WAS delighted that Jesus had agreed to meet him. "Now I can find out for myself whether or not he's twisting our traditional teaching," he said to himself. "I think I can safely say that few understand the Law better than I do."

He arrived and asked his question: "Teacher – what must I do to have eternal life?"

Jesus knew that the man was a scholar. "What do the Scriptures say?" he asked in reply.

"Ah," said the rabbi, "the great summary of the Law:

"'Love the Lord your God with all your heart, with all your soul, with all your strength, and with all your mind' is the first part, and then 'Love your neighbour as you love yourself'."

"That's the right answer," said Jesus.

The rabbi was dismayed. He hadn't probed Jesus' teaching one bit. "But it's not that simple," he protested. "Who is my neighbour?"

Jesus replied with a story.

"There was once a man who was going from Jerusalem to Jericho. In a wild and lonely spot, robbers attacked him. They stole all he had and left him for dead in the road.

"It so happened that a priest from the Temple was going that way. He saw the man and cringed away. Maybe the man was dead. He wouldn't be able to do his work at the Temple if he started dealing with a corpse.

"He tried not to look as he hurried by.

"How long must the man have been left drifting in and out of nightmares? At last someone else came along the road – a Levite, bustling along to do his work at the Temple.

"'Oh dear,' he thought. He went closer to look at the man. 'Oh dear,' he said aloud. He hesitated. What should he do? What were the consequences of his choices? Then he made up his mind, and hurried on past.

"At last another man came along the road. A Samaritan."

The rabbi glared at Jesus. The first two passers-by each had important jobs at the Temple in Jerusalem. The Samaritans had a different place of worship. They had little respect for the Jewish tradition. The words "Samaritan" and "foreign scum" tended to go together.

Jesus continued. "The Samaritan saw the injured man and felt sorry for him. He went over and tended his wounds. Then he lifted the man onto his own donkey and took him to an inn, where he took care of him.

"In the morning he had to travel on. 'Here is money,' he said to the innkeeper, 'for you to take care of the poor man. If it costs more, I'll pay the extra next time I come.'

"Now," said Jesus, "which of the three was a neighbour to the man in need?"

The rabbi actually did know the Jewish law very well. "The one who was kind to him," he said.

"Now you go and do the same," said Jesus.

The Great Feast

Luke 14:1-24

THE RABBI HOPED he was not making a mistake. "I'm proud to be a Pharisee," he said to himself. "Set apart — that's what the name means. Set apart from everything that might spoil the purity of our traditions.

"And yet I have invited that young rabbi Jesus to join some of my very important friends. Let's hope the event is a success."

Almost as soon as the guests had gathered, there was an incident. A man with badly swollen limbs came in and asked Jesus to heal him. To do so would be breaking the sabbath rules about rest. But Jesus did heal him.

He turned to face the disapproving stares.

"If you had a child — or even an ox — fall into a well on the sabbath, would you not pull them out at once?" asked Jesus. No one would answer.

Then it was time to go to the table. People jostled for the best seats, and Jesus chatted to the host.

Jesus seemed to be suggesting that he would have done better to invite strangers who were poor and in need rather than friends who were comfortably off. The host tried to shrug the comment off. Then Jesus told a story.

"There was once a man who decided to give a great feast. He invited many people.

"When everything was ready he sent his servant to tell the guests it was time to come.

"One by one they began to make excuses.

"'I've just bought some land. I must go and inspect it.'

"'I've got some new oxen. I need to go and try them out.'

"'I'm so sorry: I've just got married.'

"When the servant reported that his guests were too busy, the man was furious.

"'Go into the town and find other guests. I want the poor, the disabled, and those who are unable to work,' he said.

"They all came, delighted to have been asked. 'There's still room for more,' said the servant.

"'Then go into the countryside and find more!' declared the man. 'I want my house to be full. That other lot – they won't get a taste of all the good things on offer.'"

The Lost Sheep

Luke 15:1-7

THE RABBIS AND the Pharisees grew increasingly suspicious of Jesus.

"Just look at the kinds of rabble he welcomes!" they exclaimed to one another.

"Tax collectors, for example: nearly all are fiddling the sums so they can rake in more for themselves; and that's to say nothing of the fact that they betray their own people by working for the Romans."

"And there are all kinds of people who have no place in decent society. Jesus has no hesitation in sitting down at the table with them as friends."

Jesus told a story.

"Suppose you were a shepherd, with a hundred sheep. Suppose that one day you could only count ninety-nine.

"What would you do? You'd leave the ninety-nine safely in the pasture and go to look for the one that was lost. You wouldn't abandon it just because it had run off: you'd carry it home as if it were the most precious one in the flock.

"Once you'd got the creature home, you'd call to the neighbours and tell them to come over. 'Come on, let's have a party! I've found my lost sheep.'

"There is more joy in heaven over one wrongdoer who comes back to God than in ninety-nine respectable people who don't need to."

The Lost Son

Luke 15:11-32

FOR THE PHARISEES, the most important thing was keeping the Law faultlessly. By contrast, Jesus told his followers that those who confessed their faults to God would find forgiveness and blessing.

"Once," said Jesus, "there was a man who had two sons. The younger was growing up, and he had a dream he wanted to follow.

"'Father,' he said, 'I know that I will inherit my share of what you own one day; but I want it now, so I can go and live the life I choose.'

"He pleaded and begged until his father gave way. Then he sold his property and went off to a city far away to enjoy everything that money could buy.

"Until his money ran out. Then the harvest failed and the price of food shot up. The young man needed a job, but work was hard to find. He ended up as a farm worker in a field of pigs.

"'I'm starving,' he sighed to himself. 'I could eat this pigswill. My father always gave his workers decent food.'

"That's when the idea came to him. 'I could go back to my father. I'll admit that I've done the wrong thing and ask if he'll give me a job.'

"He didn't feel proud: he merely felt determined as he began the long journey home. He was wondering if he could just see his old home in the distance when he heard someone running toward him.

"It was his father! 'My dear, dear boy!' cried the old man, and he threw his arms around his son.

" 'I'm sorry,' began the young man. 'I know I've let you down and that I've let God down. I don't deserve to be treated as your son, but I'd be grateful for a job.'

"His father wasn't listening.

" 'Hurry,' he called to his servants. 'Get some fine clothes out for my boy.

" 'And get the best young calf ready to roast. We're going to have a party!'

"The elder son was working in the fields. As he trudged home, he heard the music and dancing and asked a servant what was going on.

"What he heard made him so furious he wouldn't even come indoors.

"The father went out to plead with him; the son replied with a scowl.

" 'I've spent years slaving for you, doing whatever you asked. And what did I get? Nothing! Not even a festive meal with my friends. Yet my good-for-nothing brother comes back and you splurge on a lavish celebration.'

" 'My dear boy,' said the father. 'Everything I have is yours. But we have to celebrate. Your brother was dead to us. Now he is alive again. We thought he was lost. Now he is found.' "

The Pharisee and the Tax Collector

Luke 18:9-14

SMUG. THAT WAS a good word to describe some of Jesus' listeners. They had no time for his message about God forgiving those who went astray. They were proud of how strictly they obeyed all God's laws.

Jesus told a story.

"Two men went to the Temple to pray.

"The Pharisee stood apart as he raised his arms and said this: 'Thank you, God, that I am not greedy, dishonest, or unfaithful in marriage as others are – men like that tax collector over there. I fast twice a week as a sign of my obedience to your laws, and give you a tenth of all I earn.'

"The tax collector stayed at the back, his head bowed in shame. 'God, have mercy on me, a sinner,' was all he said.

"It was he who went home truly at peace with God," said Jesus. "God will bless those who humbly confess their faults, and humble those who are proud."

Jesus and the Children

Mark 10:13-15

ONE DAY, SOME people brought their children to Jesus.

"We'd like him to say a little blessing prayer for them," they explained to the disciples.

The disciples shook their heads. "You can see for yourselves that he has crowds of people to deal with," they said. "Some of the most important rabbis there have come to discuss serious matters."

Jesus saw what was going on.

"You still don't understand, do you?" Jesus scolded his friends. "Let the children come to me, and don't ever try to stop them.

"The kingdom of heaven belongs to such as these. If you don't come to God's kingdom with childlike trust, you won't be allowed in."

Then he gathered the children in his arms and blessed them.

The Rich Young Man

Mark 10:17-31

THE YOUNG MAN ran eagerly up to Jesus.

"Good teacher," he asked, "please tell me what I must do to receive eternal life."

"Why do you call me good?" asked Jesus. "No one except God can be called good. You know God's commandments: do not murder; be faithful in marriage; do not steal; do not tell lies to get someone else into trouble; do not cheat; respect your mother and your father."

"I know!" agreed the young man. "I've known those laws and obeyed them all my life."

Jesus could tell that the young man was eager to do what was right. He could also see what was holding him back from becoming a faithful disciple.

"Go and sell all you have," he told him. "Give the money to the poor, and then come and follow me. Then you will be rich in heaven."

The young man hesitated. He looked down at his fine robe and looked back at Jesus.

"I'll… I'll have to think about that," said the young man. Then he plodded slowly away.

Jesus looked at his disciples.

"It's easier for a camel to get through the eye of a needle than for a rich person to enter God's kingdom," he said. "In fact, it is only because of God's kindness that anyone can be part of it."

A Blind Man Healed

John 9:1–41; 10:1–21

As Jesus was walking along the road, he saw a man who had been born blind.

"Why did that happen?" the disciples asked. "Was it his wrongdoing, or the wrongdoing of his parents?"

"It is not about wrongdoing," replied Jesus. "Yet because of his blindness, he will learn of God's power. While I am in the world, I am light for the world."

Then he spat on the ground and made some mud, which he spread on the man's eyes.

"Go and wash in the Pool of Siloam," explained Jesus.

The man went. As he opened his eyes, he shrieked with joy.

"I can see!" he cried. "I can see!"

Friends and neighbours came rushing to find out what was going on. They were astonished to see that the man who had spent his life begging was now walking around, laughing and happy.

"Jesus healed me!" the man explained.

The local Pharisees were alarmed at the news. "So how do you think Jesus did this?" they asked the man.

"He's a prophet," came the simple reply.

"Jesus is not a prophet," whispered the Pharisees among themselves. "Let's ask the man's parents if he really was blind or if this is some kind of pretence."

The man's parents were quite clear that their son had always been blind. They didn't dare say more: they knew anyone who seemed to believe in Jesus would be excluded from the synagogue.

"Just listen to the facts!" said the man.

"Once I was blind; now I see."

The Pharisees did exactly what the man's parents feared: they told the young man he was no longer part of the worshipping community. He didn't care. He went and followed Jesus.

Some Pharisees were watching as the man came and declared his faith.

"Do you understand?" asked Jesus. "I came into this world to judge it: those who were blind will see, and those who could see will become blind."

"Surely you are not saying that we are blind!" argued the Pharisees.

"The problem is," explained Jesus, "that you claim to see everything very clearly... but do you really?"

"If you see someone climbing over the wall into a sheepfold, you know he's up to no good. The shepherd goes in through the gate, and the sheep recognize him and follow him.

"I'm like that: I am the gate for the sheep. I have come to give my followers life in abundance.

"I am the good shepherd: I am willing to die to save my sheep from danger. That is what God wants me to do; that is what I am willing to do."

The Pharisees shook their heads. "The man's mad," they muttered.

Others disagreed. "A madman wouldn't be able to heal as Jesus does," they said.

Lazarus and His Sisters

John 11:1-44

JESUS HAD GOOD friends living near Jerusalem: a man named Lazarus and his sisters Mary and Martha. They all respected his teaching and were delighted whenever he came to stay in their home, in the town of Bethany.

However, the religious leaders in Jerusalem were growing very suspicious of Jesus and his teaching, and the time came when he felt it wiser to leave the city and go to a place beyond the River Jordan.

While he was there, Lazarus fell ill. The sisters sent Jesus a message to tell him.

"This isn't going to end in his death," Jesus said. "What is about to happen will bring glory to God and to the Son of God."

Even so, Jesus waited two days before he announced to his disciples that they must go back to the region of Jerusalem.

"Don't be foolish!" they warned him. "The people there are after your blood."

"Our friend Lazarus has fallen asleep," said Jesus. "I must go and wake him."

"He'll wake up soon enough!" they protested.

Jesus shook his head. "I mean, he's dead. But don't be sad. Something good will come of it."

As Jesus arrived in the town, Martha came rushing out to greet him. "If only you'd come sooner," she wept, "though I know that God will give you whatever you ask for."

"Your brother will rise to life again," Jesus told her.

"I know," she sobbed, "at the resurrection, on the last day."

"I am the resurrection and the life," said Jesus. "Do you believe that?"

"Yes I do," said Martha. "I believe you are the messiah, the Son of God."

Martha hurried back to the house to tell Mary that Jesus had
arrived. Mary rushed out to find him, and everyone who had come
to comfort her followed.

When Jesus saw the grieving crowd, he asked to be taken to the
grave. It was a cave, with a stone door rolled in place.

"Open it up," requested Jesus.

Martha shook her head. "He's been buried four days," she said.
"The body will smell dreadful."

Jesus insisted. He said a prayer to God in front of
the open tomb and then cried, "Lazarus, come out."

The man that everyone thought was dead came walking out,
wrapped as a corpse.

"Untie him," said Jesus. "Set him free to live."

The Tax Collector and the Tree

Luke 19:1-10

JESUS' ARRIVAL OFTEN caused a stir. In the busy town of Jericho, the crowds gathered in no time. Even the chief tax collector, Zacchaeus, wanted to see the famous teacher.

"Why is he trying to push to the front?" grumbled someone. "He's not interested in religious teaching as far as I know."

"Yeah, he's only interested in money: and getting his hands on as much of yours and mine as he can."

"He's totally dishonest."

"He collaborates with the Romans. Nasty piece of work."

No one would let Zacchaeus through to the front.

"But I can't see... I'm too short." Zacchaeus was fretting that he would miss his chance of catching a glimpse of Jesus. Then he had an idea. He ran ahead of the crowd and climbed a tree. Now he had a perfect view. Jesus was going to come right underneath.

Jesus did come that way... and he stopped. "Zacchaeus," he called. "Come down. I want to stay at your house."

Zacchaeus was astonished and delighted all at once. He hardly heard the crowd grumbling about why the famous rabbi had chosen to dine

with the man they all hated.

Nor did Jesus seem to
care what the crowd thought.
He wanted to speak to Zacchaeus, and
that was what he was going to do.

Whatever Jesus said certainly made a difference.
When the meal was over, Zacchaeus stood up and made
an announcement. "I'm going to change my life around.
I'm going to give half of what I have to the poor, and
where I've cheated people, I shall repay four times the amount."

Jesus was pleased. "Showing people that they need to change
their ways and get on the right path is just what I came to do,"
he said.

Riding to Jerusalem

Luke 18:31-34; 19:28-40

JESUS KNEW THAT the religious authorities in Jerusalem had made up their mind to silence him. They were looking for some charge on which they could have him condemned to death. The matter could not be avoided. Boldly Jesus led his disciples to the city.

When they were nearly there, he sent his disciples to fetch a donkey colt. "If anyone challenges you, simply say, 'The master needs it,'" he told them.

It all happened as predicted. The disciples threw their cloaks over the colt's back and helped Jesus to get on. As Jesus set along the road people began to notice.

Some threw their cloaks on the road to make a processional way.
Others cut branches and waved them aloft.

"God bless the king! God bless God's chosen king!"

"Praise God! Hosanna in the highest!"

There were some Pharisees in the crowd, and they were furious
that Jesus was letting his followers greet him as if he were the
messiah.

"How dare you let your followers behave like this?"
they exclaimed.

"Even if they said nothing," replied Jesus,
"the stones themselves would shout out
the truth."

87

In the Temple Courtyard

Luke 19:41-48

As Jesus came closer to the city of Jerusalem, he could see its strong walls. He could glimpse the Temple building rising above them, its marble gleaming in the sunshine. The sight reduced him to tears.

"It's so sad," he wept. "Jerusalem simply does not know what is needed for peace. The time is coming when all of it will be caught up in a rebellion and destroyed."

He rode on up the hill and through the city gate. As he walked into the Temple courtyard, what he saw made him angry. It looked like a market. Some stallholders were selling the sheep and doves to be bought and offered as sacrifices in worship. Others were changing money into the special Temple coins that people could give as offerings. They had turned the worship of God into a business, run for profit.

"Get out!" he told the stallholders. He began to overturn the tables. "Our Scriptures tell us that the Temple is to be a place of prayer.

"You have turned it into a den of thieves."

The chief priests and the teachers of the Law looked on grimly. "We have to get rid of him," they agreed. "We'll have to find out where he goes at night, when the feeble-minded, adoring crowds aren't around, hanging on his every word.

"We are all agreed: Jesus is a troublemaker."

The Tenants in the Vineyard

Luke 20:1-16

NOW THAT HE was in Jerusalem, Jesus went to the Temple to preach his message. It was quite usual for rabbis to do such a thing: but the Temple authorities were furious that Jesus was doing so.

"What right do you have to say the things you do?" they asked.

The only answer he gave was a story.

"There was once a man who planted a vineyard and let it out to tenants. He himself went away for a long time.

"When it was time to harvest the grapes, the man sent a servant to collect his share. The tenants beat him and sent him away.

"The man sent another servant and the same thing happened. When a third servant returned, bruised, bloodied, and empty handed, he made a new plan.

"'I will send my son,' he said to himself. 'They will surely respect him.'

"When the tenants saw the son, they made a wicked plan. 'This is the owner's son! Let's kill him, and the vineyard will be ours.'

"Now here's a question," said Jesus. "What will the owner do when he finds out his son has been killed? He will come and punish the wrongdoers and hand his vineyard over to other tenants."

A Marked Man

Matthew 26:6-16

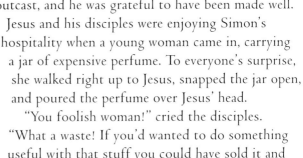

AMONG JESUS' FRIENDS in Bethany was a man named Simon. Jesus had cured him of a skin disease so horrible that it had made him an outcast, and he was grateful to have been made well.

Jesus and his disciples were enjoying Simon's hospitality when a young woman came in, carrying a jar of expensive perfume. To everyone's surprise, she walked right up to Jesus, snapped the jar open, and poured the perfume over Jesus' head.

"You foolish woman!" cried the disciples. "What a waste! If you'd wanted to do something useful with that stuff you could have sold it and given the money to the poor."

"What was the point of all that drama, all that extravagance?"

Jesus interrupted. "Leave her alone," he said. "What she has done is good and beautiful. It's only what someone would do to prepare a body for burial — so now I'm truly ready even to face death.

"As for the poor: there will always be poor people in need of your help, but you won't always have me. You can be sure that wherever my message is preached, the story of her generosity and love will be remembered."

One of the disciples remained thoroughly disapproving. The event shocked him into action. His name was Judas Iscariot, and he went to speak to the chief priests.

"I know you're trying to get Jesus arrested," he said. "What will you give me if I arrange for that to happen in a secret location?"

"Ah!" came the reply. "We see you've come to your senses – not worried that your former friends will see you as a traitor. Useful, very useful."

And so for thirty silver coins Judas agreed to tip them off about where to find Jesus alone.

93

A New Commandment

John 13:1-35

IT WAS THE day before the Passover festival. Jesus knew that he was nearing the end of his time on earth. He wanted to prepare his disciples for all that lay ahead.

They came together to share a meal. Jesus took off his coat and wrapped a towel around his waist as an apron. Then he fetched water, and began to wash his disciples' dusty feet.

Peter objected. "You're not a servant and I'm not going to let you act like one. Leave my feet as they are."

"Then you won't be a disciple of mine," replied Jesus.

Peter was startled. "Then wash me all over!" he declared.

"That won't be necessary," said Jesus. "All of you are clean enough... except one."

When everyone was once again gathered around the table, Jesus explained what he had done. "You call me your teacher, you accept my authority, and that is right.

"I have just acted as your servant, and that is how you should treat one another.

"But there's something worrying me: one of you has lost his trust in me. One of you is going to betray me."

The disciples were puzzled. Peter wanted to know who the traitor was. He motioned to John to ask.

Jesus whispered the answer. "The one to whom I pass some bread. Watch."

Shortly after, Jesus passed some bread to Judas Iscariot. "Off you go," he said simply.

Judas hurried away almost unnoticed. Everyone thought he was on some errand.

"It's nearly the end for me now," sighed Jesus. "Now I am giving you a new commandment. Love one another. As I have loved you, so you must love one another. Your love will show the world that you are my disciples."

The Last Supper

Mark 14:22-25

THE PASSOVER MEAL was a time to remember. In days long past, so the Scriptures said, the nation had been slaves in Egypt. God had chosen a man named Moses to lead the people to freedom. He worked many wonders to show he had power from God, but the king of Egypt would not let his slaves go to a land of their own.

Then came the first Passover night: Moses told the people to kill a lamb to eat and to daub some of its blood on their doors. The blood would be a sign for the angel of death to pass over their homes. In the homes of the Egyptians, death would strike the firstborn.

All this came true. As the people made the journey to a new land, God made a covenant with them: God would be their God and they would be God's own people, obeying faithfully the laws God had given to Moses.

While the disciples were eating the festival meal, Jesus took a piece of bread and said a prayer of thanks. Then he broke the bread and gave it to his friends. "Take it," he said. "This is my body."

Next, he took a cup of wine and said a prayer of thanks. He handed the cup to them saying, "This is my blood which is poured out for many, the sure sign that the covenant is real and true. I will never again drink this wine until I drink the new wine of God's kingdom."

The Garden of Gethsemane

Mark 14:26-42

AFTER THE MEAL, Jesus and his disciples left the room and went out of Jerusalem. They crossed the valley to the Mount of Olives.

"You will all desert me soon," sighed Jesus. "I will be killed, and you will scatter like sheep."

"I won't run," insisted Peter. "I'll stay with you whatever the rest do."

Jesus shook his head. "Before the cock crows the dawn, you will deny knowing me three times."

They reached the olive grove of Gethsemane. Jesus asked Peter, James, and John to come with him, saying that he needed time to pray.

As the four walked on, Jesus began to tremble and weep. "I'm almost crushed with sorrow tonight," he said. "Stay here and keep watch, please."

Then he went a little further off and prayed. "O God, do not let me suffer. Please find another way for your will to be done. Yet – not what I want, but what you want."

He returned to find his three closest disciples asleep. "Simon Peter," he chided. "Couldn't you stay awake even one hour?

"Come on: stay alert. Pray that you won't have to face the hard times that lie ahead for me."

A second time he went off to pray; a second time he had to rouse the three disciples.

When he returned from prayer a third time and found them sleeping, he was more anxious than ever.

"Wake up. The time has come. The one who will betray me has returned and we must go."

A Dark Night for Peter

Mark 14:43-54, 66-72

JESUS WAS STILL speaking when Judas Iscariot emerged from the shadows.

"Teacher!" he cried, as he stepped forward and kissed Jesus, as was the custom.

From behind, a crowd of men armed with clubs and swords rushed to overpower Jesus.

"Did you have to come and get me this way?" Jesus asked. "You didn't dare when you saw me in the Temple, did you? Even though I was there day after day!"

There was a brief scuffle as the disciples attempted to fight back on behalf of their leader, but then they all ran off.

Jesus was taken to the high priest's house. Peter followed at a distance. He mingled with the guards and servants who were busy in the courtyard and took a place by the fire.

A servant girl came by and noticed Peter. "You," she said. "You were with Jesus of Nazareth."

"I don't know what you're talking about," Peter snapped. Even so, he moved to a quieter spot. A cock crowed.

The servant girl passed him again. "See that man," she said to the other servants. "He's one of the Jesus lot."

Peter curled his lip contemptuously. "You want to watch what you say, trying to get innocent bystanders into trouble."

In spite of his anger, the servants began to whisper among themselves. A man came and pointed his finger. "You are one

of Jesus' lot and you've got the same Galilean accent," he accused.

"God strike me if I'm lying; I don't know what you mean!" cried Peter.

The cock crowed a second time. A pale shard of light lit the dawn sky.

Peter remembered Jesus' words: "Before the cock crows twice, you will say three times that you do not know me."

He turned and slunk away, feeling guilty and ashamed.

Trial at Night

Mark 14:53-64

THE ARMED MEN who arrested Jesus took him to the high priest's house in Jerusalem. All the religious leaders had assembled there: priests, elders, and rabbis. The whole Council was eager to convict the preacher from Galilee.

"Bring in the first witness," announced the high priest. A man who had agreed to denounce Jesus came and told a damning story.

"Next witness," called the high priest. The next to speak also gave evidence of wrong things Jesus had said and done. However, it didn't fit with what the first witness had said. The religious leaders shifted uneasily.

More witnesses were brought. Now the stories really were conflicting. Perhaps not everyone was telling the truth. Perhaps no one was.

The high priest called for silence. "Jesus," he said. "You have heard the accusations. What do you say about them?"

Jesus did not answer.

"Answer me this," demanded the high priest. "Are you the messiah, the Son of the Blessed God?"

"I am," replied Jesus. "You will see heaven bear witness to me."

The high priest exploded with rage. "We don't need any more witnesses," he cried. "You all heard him claim that he is the representative of God. That is blasphemy. What is your verdict on this insolent pretender?"

"Guilty," replied those assembled. "He should die for his crime."

Condemned

Mark 15:1-20

THE AUTHORITY TO pass a sentence of death in Jerusalem belonged to one man only: Pontius Pilate, the Roman governor. The religious leaders asked for Jesus to be condemned.

Pilate listened to their arguments. Then he questioned Jesus. "I am told you claim to be king of the Jews," he said. "Is this true?"

"It is as you say," replied Jesus.

Pilate was baffled. He asked more questions, but the prisoner said nothing. Meanwhile, the crowds were gathering outside.

There was a custom that the governor would free a prisoner at Passover. Pilate went to the balcony.

"Do you want me to free the king of the Jews?" he asked.

He had no idea how quickly the religious authorities had been working. They had stirred up the crowd to ask for another: Barabbas, in prison for rebellion and murder.

"What do you want me to do with the one you call the king of the Jews, then?" asked Pilate.

"Crucify him!" came the reply. "Nail him to a cross."

Pilate's main concern was public order. He set Barabbas free and he handed Jesus over to the guard.

The soldiers laughed when they saw their prisoner's crime.

"A king, eh? We've got a nice purple cloak for kings to wear. And here's your crown. The emperor's one is laurel, but we could only find thorns."

They dressed Jesus in mock finery and bowed down.

"Long live the king of the Jews," they said. "Oh – bad news. We have to execute you. Not such a long and glorious reign after all."

"Now hurry up: get your own clothes back on. You don't want to be late for your own funeral."

The Crucifixion

John 19:17-30

THE SOLDIERS LOADED a wooden cross onto Jesus' shoulders and led him to be crucified, along with two other prisoners. At the place of execution they hammered iron nails through Jesus' hands and feet to fasten him to the cross. Pilate had prepared a notice of his crime that was fastened above him:

"*Jesus: king of the Jews*"

The religious leaders were dismayed.

"That's not quite right," they told Pilate. "It should say, 'This man said, I am the king of the Jews.'"

Pilate dismissed them impatiently. "What I've written stays that way," he snapped.

As Jesus hung on the cross, the soldiers took his clothes and shared them out among themselves, gambling to see who should get the robe that was woven in one piece.

Nearby, Jesus' mother wept, while a huddle of women and one of Jesus' disciples tried to comfort her.

Jesus called out to his mother: "You see John there – he will be your son now.

"John: please take care of my mother as you would your own."

Jesus knew he had done everything he had been born to do. "I'm thirsty," he sighed.

Someone lifted a wine-soaked sponge to his lips. Jesus drank the wine and said, "It is finished."

Then he bowed his head and died.

Death and Resurrection

Matthew 27:57 - 28:8

THE DAY OF Jesus' crucifixion was drawing to an end. A rich man
from the town of Arimathea, a man named Joseph, hurried to where
the soldiers were taking down the crosses and the pale corpses
nailed to them.

"You must be the man who's going to take the body," said one
of the guards. "The orders from Pilate just got here."

Joseph nodded. He had arranged for the body to be carried to a rock-cut tomb that he had bought for his own eventual burial. Two of Jesus' followers – Mary Magdalene and another Mary – watched tearfully as servants placed the body inside and rolled the stone door across the tomb's entrance.

The next day was the sabbath, the weekly day of rest. Even so, the religious authorities were anxious that the Jesus affair be properly finished. They went to Pilate:

"Jesus used to tell his followers he would rise from the dead. We must make sure they don't go and steal his body and then start spreading rumours about such a thing."

"Go and make the tomb as secure as you can," Pilate said. "I'll arrange for a couple of soldiers to keep watch over it."

Very early, on the Sunday morning, the two Marys went back to the tomb. Suddenly the earth shook. The women saw an angel roll the stone away. The guards fainted with fright.

"Don't be afraid," said the angel to the women. "Jesus has been raised to life. Go and tell his disciples that he is going to Galilee and will see you all there."

The women gasped. What news they had to tell!

The Stranger in the Garden

John 20:11-18

MARY MAGDALENE COULD not bear to leave the tomb. She stood outside, weeping uncontrollably. There was only one thing she was sure of: Jesus' tomb stood open; Jesus' body was not in it.

She peered in one more time, just to make sure. Inside were two angels, dressed in white, seated where the body should have been.

"Why are you crying?" they asked.

"They have taken away the body of my Lord and I don't know where they have put him," she sobbed.

She turned around and saw someone outside. She thought it must be the gardener.

"O Sir!" she pleaded. "Was it you who took the body away? If it was, please tell me where you have put him, so I can go there."

The man stepped forward and said simply, "Mary."

At once she recognized Jesus.

"*Rabboni!*" she gasped. "Teacher."

"Don't try to hold on to me," said Jesus. "Go and tell my disciples that I am returning to my Father and their Father, my God and their God."

"I will!" exclaimed Mary. "I'll go at once!"

On the Road to Emmaus

Luke 24:13-35

SUNDAY MORNING HAD brought tumultuous news to Jesus' disciples, and the rumours of it spread through Jerusalem. In the evening, a couple of Jesus' followers left the city for their home in Emmaus. They were talking about everything they had heard when a stranger joined them.

"What are you talking about?" asked the man.

"You must have heard," said the one named Cleopas. "You know

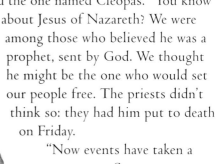

about Jesus of Nazareth? We were among those who believed he was a prophet, sent by God. We thought he might be the one who would set our people free. The priests didn't think so: they had him put to death on Friday.

"Now events have taken a strange turn. Some women went to Jesus' tomb this morning and came back saying they saw angels, that Jesus is alive."

"Ah," said the stranger. "This sounds like the promises in Scripture coming true."

As the three walked on together, he began explaining all about
how the messiah had been foretold in the ancient books and what
would happen when he came.

When they reached Emmaus, the couple wanted to go on
listening. "Come and stay with us," they offered the stranger. "It's
too dark to travel on."

As the three sat down to eat, the stranger took the bread and said
the prayer of thanks before breaking it into pieces and sharing it
around.

Then the couple recognized who it was who had been talking to
them – but he had vanished.

"That was Jesus!" the couple agreed. "We must go to Jerusalem
and tell everyone."

Thomas

John 20:19-31

SUNDAY'S DAWN HAD brought the faithful disciples news of Jesus' resurrection. As the sun set, they gathered together and locked the doors securely, afraid that Jesus' enemies might now be looking for them.

To their amazement, Jesus came and stood among them and gave the customary greeting.

"Peace be with you."

He showed them his hands and the wound in his side. The marks were clear proof that he was none other than their beloved leader.

114

"I am sending you out into the world in the power of God's Spirit," he told them. "Those whom you forgive God will forgive also."

One of the disciples, Thomas, was not with the others when this happened. He did not believe them when they said they had seen Jesus.

"I'm not going to fall for this nonsense unless I see Jesus for myself and the marks of the crucifixion," he declared.

A week later the disciples were again together in a locked room. Jesus came and spoke to Thomas. "Here I am: you can touch my hands, feel my side. Stop doubting and believe."

Thomas simply replied, "My Lord and my God."

"You believe because you have seen," said Jesus. "God will pour blessings on those who believe without seeing."

By Lake Galilee

John 21:1-19

A GROUP OF JESUS' disciples had returned to their home region of Galilee. Peter decided to return to his old life.

"I'm going fishing," he said.

"We'll come too," said the others.

They all went out in a boat together, but they caught nothing. As the sun rose, they headed back for shore.

"Didn't you young men catch anything?" called someone from the beach.

"No, we didn't," they called back.

"Then throw your net out on the right," called the stranger.

They did so, and it quickly filled with more fish than they could haul aboard.

Suddenly John whispered to Peter. "The man on the shore: it's Jesus!"

"Is it? Then I've got to speak to him – take my place at the net!"

Peter stripped off his tunic and swam the short distance to where Jesus was. The others sailed the boat in, still pulling the loaded net through the water.

Jesus was waiting beside a charcoal fire. He had some bread with him. "Let's cook some of those fish," he said, and he prepared a meal for them all.

Then Jesus took Peter to one side. "Simon Peter, son of John, do you love me more than the other disciples?" he asked.

"Yes I do," came the reply. "You know I do."

"Then take care of my lambs," said Jesus. There was a pause. Then Jesus asked his question again.

"Simon, son of John, do you love me?"

"Yes," came the reply. "You know I do."

"Take care of my sheep."

A third time Jesus asked, and a third time Peter gave the same answer.

"Then take care of my sheep," said Jesus. "Whatever the cost, whatever the danger, follow me."

The Ascension

Luke 24:44-53 and Acts 1:8-11

JESUS KNEW THAT he did not have long to spend with his disciples. He used the time to explain to them that he was indeed the messiah promised in the Scriptures: how it was foretold that he would die and rise again.

"Now the time has come to preach the message you have heard me give: that people should repent of having turned away from God. When they do, they will find forgiveness and a welcome.

"You must spread this message – first in Jerusalem and then to all the world. God will give you power from heaven to strengthen you for the task."

Together they went to Bethany. Jesus said a blessing prayer and then he was taken up to heaven.

The disciples were still peering upwards when two men dressed in white came and stood beside them.

"Why are you looking at the sky?" they asked. "Jesus has gone to heaven. One day, he will return in the same way that you have seen him go."

The Day of Pentecost

Acts 2

FIFTY DAYS AFTER Passover came the harvest festival of Pentecost. All those who believed in Jesus were together in a room in Jerusalem.

Suddenly they heard a noise like a strong wind blowing through the house. Golden flames danced above them, scattering darkness and fear together.

"It's just as Jesus said," someone remarked. "God is filling us with the power of the Holy Spirit to go and spread the message of God's kingdom."

They all danced out into the street, laughing and chattering.

The streets were crowded, with pilgrims coming to the festival from all over the empire.

"Did you hear that?" they began to say to each other.

"These are local people, yet they're speaking our language."

"And ours too!"

"Is it a miracle… or have they just been drinking?"

Peter found a place to stand where he could address the crowd.

"People of Jerusalem, listen to this. We're not drunk – it's only nine o'clock in the morning. Rather, it is God's Holy Spirit, giving us the courage and the words to tell you all about Jesus. He was the messiah – God's promised king.

"What you must do is turn to God. He will forgive your wrongdoing and make you his children."

Many who heard the news on that day believed it and became followers of Jesus.

Since that time, there have many more; and still today people come to faith and find blessing.

Where Jesus Lived

THE LAND WHERE Jesus lived is on the eastern shore of the Mediterranean Sea.

People grew crops that thrived in the warm, dry summers: olives, grapes, barley, and vegetables. Shepherds led their flocks of sheep and goats to graze the hillsides, and cattle were raised on lusher pastures. Many of Jesus' stories refer to everyday activities such as these.

Jesus' birth is described as being in Bethlehem. This was the town where, hundreds of years earlier, the nation's great king David had been born. It is something that identifies Jesus as the true successor to David.

Jerusalem was the city claimed by David as his capital. It was also where David's son, Solomon, first built a Temple. In the time of Jesus, a glittering new Temple had been built on the same site by order of the local king, Herod the Great.

Jesus himself was raised in the region of Galilee, in the town of Nazareth. When the local people rejected him as a teacher, he moved to Capernaum, a fishing village on the shore of Lake Galilee. Most of his teaching took place in the towns and villages around Galilee, although on several occasions he travelled south to Jericho, Bethany, and Jerusalem. It was just outside Jerusalem's walls that he was crucified.

MEDITERRANEAN SEA

Caesarea Philippi

GALILEE

Capernaum

Cana

Magdala

LAKE GALILEE

Nazareth

SAMARIA

RIVER JORDAN

JUDEA

Jericho

Jerusalem

Bethany

Bethlehem

DEAD SEA

Index

Note: where a subject in this index occurs on both left and right of a double page spread, only the left hand page number is given.